THE C.A.R.E METHOD

Transformative Coaching for Every Generation

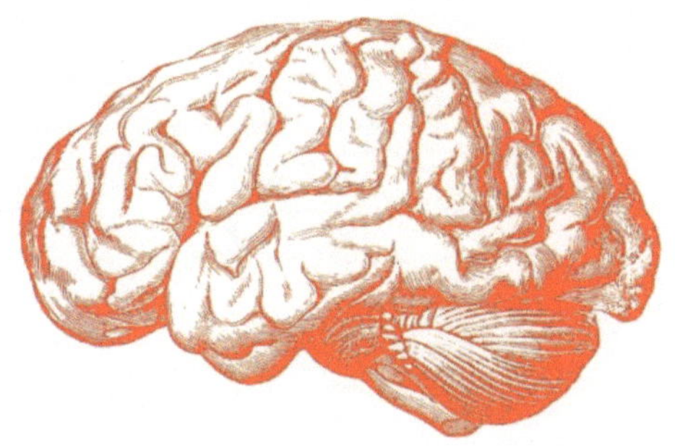

Steven L. JORDAN, SR., Ph.D
Ed.D

TABLE OF CONTENTS

FOREWORD

The C.A.R.E. Method: Transformative Coaching for Every Generation

Dr. Steven Jordan's book, "The CARE Method," offers a profound exploration of leadership development. It integrates the depth of his unique methodology with the foundational principles of the International Coach Federation (ICF) Core Competencies. The ICF Core Competencies are structured into four categories: Foundation, Co-Creating the Relationship, Communicating Effectively, and Cultivating Learning and Growth. These competencies emphasize ethical practices, a coaching mindset, active listening, trust-building, and fostering client growth.

Dr. Jordan's approach aligns seamlessly with these competencies, particularly in emphasizing empathy, active listening, and ethical standards. He underscores the importance of a coaching mindset that is open, curious, and client-centered, which is essential for effective coaching and leadership. His comprehensive guide provides readers with actionable strategies to enhance their leadership capabilities while fostering a supportive and effective coaching environment.

For those willing to delve into this script, "The CARE Method" promises to be an invaluable resource for both aspiring and seasoned leaders.

Dr. Gary Patterson, M.Div., Th.M., D.D., CCUCH, MCC
CVO
Organizational Leadership Coaching® Institute,
San Antonio, Texas
Dr. Gary Patterson is a Master Certified Coach (MCC) from the International Coaching Federation (ICF) with over three decades of expertise in leadership development and training.

Introduction

"The quality of a person's life is in direct proportion to their commitment to excellence, regardless of their chosen field of endeavor."— Vince Lombardi.

This quote by American football legend Vince Lombardi holds for all of us. Our commitment to excellence dictates the quality of our lives and, in turn, influences our success. Achieving the right balance between commitment to excellence, quality of life, and success is key to productivity, efficiency, effectiveness, and overall success.

However, the world has drastically changed since Lombardi's time. We are in the midst of a technological revolution, with a new generation of professionals eager to make their mark. Unlike the baby boomers, Millennials and Generation Z face unique challenges. The traditional path of long-term employment with a single company is becoming rare. Today's workers seek growth, new opportunities, and a distinct professional identity amid fierce competition.

Sturt and Nordstrom highlight those new hires "intend to stay long, become part of something bigger, and produce great work." (Sturt & Nordstrom, 2016). This desire to make a noticeable difference and be exceptional is commendable. But what happens when reality doesn't match these aspirations?

When engagement decreases and excitement wanes, productivity and effectiveness suffer. Managers and leaders play a crucial role in this. Motivating and coaching employees to be their best selves is challenging but essential.

For the past thirty years, I have dedicated myself to helping others achieve a mindset of excellence. Whether working with employees, team members, or soldiers, my goal has been to inspire their belief in their abilities. Effective coaching requires understanding each individual's unique challenges and adapting strategies to meet the needs of a constantly evolving workforce.

In this eBook, I will share the coaching approaches that have proven successful when working with clients in their late twenties to early forties. You will learn tips, tricks, and insights that combine passion, excellence, and strategies into an effective playbook for developing professionals across various fields.

Each of these aspects will be explored in detail, providing

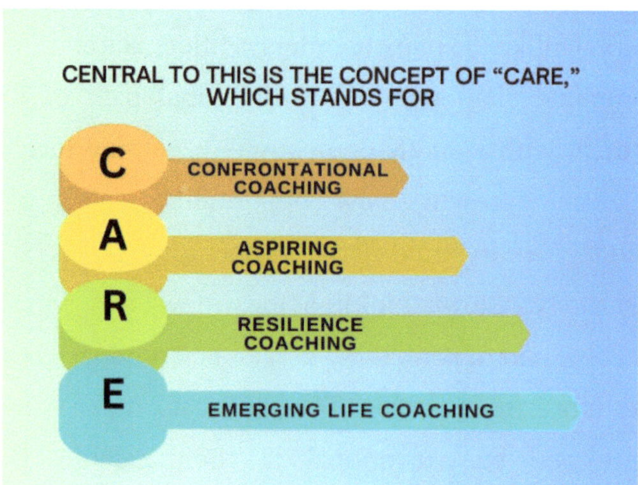

you with a comprehensive coaching strategy for today's dynamic work environment.

Using CARE will transform and improve your approach to

coaching, enabling you to help your clients achieve excellence.

Let's begin our journey together into CARE.

-Steven L. Jordan, Ph.D., Ed.D. (AKA: Dr. J)

CONFRONTATIONAL COACHING

Now, if someone—whether in your personal life or the workplace— were to tell you that your job as a coach entailed active confrontation with your clients on a daily basis, you'd probably find yourself questioning their knowledge of the field! However, it's safe to say that a little bit of confrontation can go a long way. It's not about strictly pointing out a flaw, a problem, or an issue— it's about holding someone accountable for their actions in a way that allows them to acknowledge where something went wrong so they can correct it and learn from it.

In other words, there's a big difference between a confrontation and a constructive confrontation. In this section, we'll take a deep dive into the art of aggressive coaching. We'll learn about the best ways to apply confrontational coaching strategies in your approach and discuss some instances where confrontational coaching can be best applied.

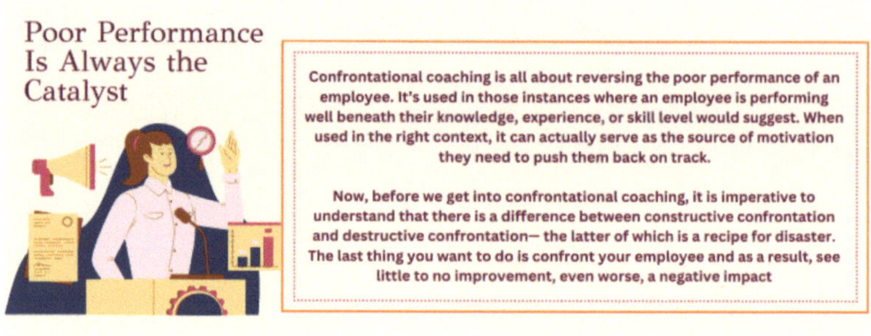

Your Employees Deserve to Know the Truth

Confrontational coaching is all about the truth—it's about

being honest with your employees about their job performance. It's about being open with them about areas for improvement while also pointing out areas where they're succeeding.

Sometimes, the truth can hurt— and when it's due to poor performance, it should sting a little. But the goal is to do it in a way that allows your employee to see what you see and to dig deep within themselves to bring their performance back up to the level where it needs to be. After all, if you didn't believe they had the potential to reach the next level, you wouldn't have hired them in the first place!

Part of being an effective leader and an effective coach is being able to recognize when confrontation is warranted and when it just isn't necessary. But once you've made that call, you need to do it the right way.

Confronting the Right Way

Confrontations can be challenging situations, and it is up to us to initiate, manage and communicate them effectively. They begin and end with us. Before confronting an employee, we must take our feelings and considerations into account. If we approach the situation with anger or frustration—emotions we may naturally feel at the time—we risk causing a conflict, which is not the goal of constructive confrontation. However, if we approach the employee with understanding and accountability, we provide them with an opportunity to reflect on their performance, identify their shortcoming, and strive for improvement.

From there, we need to trust ourselves. We need to trust our ability to coach our clients to success, and we need to trust our thoughts and feelings as the confrontation unfolds. In many situations, an employee might get defensive, and our response becomes key to navigating the situation away from a potential conflict. Take note of the word, response. Instead of reacting, you need to trust your ability to listen, empathize, and respond.

Lastly, we need to ensure the confrontation ends on a positive note. While this may not happen right off the bat, you must continue to work with your employees to ensure they take note of at least one positive outcome from the confrontation. This can range anywhere from identifying the reasons for poor performance to developing a strategy to make them a more effective worker. It can also be something as simple as giving them a chance to vent or to convey their side of the story— maybe something is going on outside of work that's affecting their performance.

You can never truly be sure of how the situation will unfold, but just knowing how to apply the approach of constructive confrontation to effectively coach your employee or client into excellence is absolutely key.

Articulating Your Point of View

As a coach, it should be safe to assume that you've developed a strong skillset that allows you to connect with people. You're more than likely to consider yourself a people person, and you've probably held some leadership position throughout your career— whether you were or are a business owner, a manager, a director, or an executive. Hopefully, clearly articulating your thoughts, your point of view, or your vision has become part of your skill set.

When it comes to constructive confrontations, nothing can be more important than having the ability to know what you want to say and being sure you say it well. There always needs to be an open and honest conversation between you and your employee. In an article on the topic, Scott suggests, "steer clear of inflammatory comments… keep to 'I' statements that present what you are experiencing without assigning blame." (Scott, n.d.). And while that's good advice, it's most important to remember there is a way to hold your employee accountable without necessarily assigning blame.

By pointing out specific situations in which your employee struggled or failed to achieve a goal, bringing in any relevant data or metrics that you may have to show you've been accurately tracking their performance, and including any relevant feedback from customers, other team members, or managers, you can help them see for themselves exactly where they stand.

While you compile this information, it would also be helpful to point out specific situations in which their performance was on par with where it should be, along with relevant data and metrics to support it. You can even point to positive customer feedback, too! Every step of the way, be clear about what you want the employee to gain from this confrontation, and ensure you build them back up with positives.

From there, you'll be engaging in the very first step of C.A.R.E Coaching.

Practical Steps for Confrontational Coaching

Step One: Preparation

- o Gather relevant performance data to support your observations.
- o Approach the conversation with constructive intent, aiming for improvement rather than criticism.
- o Anticipate possible reactions and plan your responses to maintain control of the conversation.

Step Two: Initiating the Conversation

- o Start with positives to build rapport and set a constructive tone.
- o Address specific performance issues using "I" statements to avoid placing blame (e.g., "I noticed..." rather than "You did...").
- o Maintain a calm and composed demeanor to create a safe space for open dialogue.

Step Three: Collaborative Problem-Solving:

- o Engage the employee in finding solutions by asking for their input and ideas.
- o Develop a clear, actionable plan that outlines steps for improvement.
- o Encourage open dialogue to understand their perspective and show their input is valued.

The Role of Emotional Intelligence in Confrontational Coaching

Emotional intelligence (EI) plays a crucial role in confrontational coaching. EI involves recognizing and managing one's emotions and those of others. High EI can help one navigate confrontational situations more effectively. According to Daniel Goleman, the key components of EI include self-awareness, self-regulation, motivation, empathy, and social skills.

By leveraging EI, you can approach confrontations with empathy and understanding, which helps in de-escalating potential conflicts. For example, being aware of your emotions can prevent you from reacting impulsively, while empathy allows you to see the situation from your employee's perspective, fostering a more constructive dialogue.

Integrating International Coaching Federation (ICF) Ethical Principles and Core Competencies

The International Coaching Federation (ICF) outlines several ethical principles and core competencies that are essential for effective coaching. These include maintaining the highest level of integrity and professionalism, respecting confidentiality, and promoting the client's best interests.

In confrontational coaching, these principles translate to respecting your client's dignity and autonomy, even when addressing performance issues. Core competencies such as active listening, powerful questioning, and direct communication are particularly relevant. Active listening ensures that you fully understand your employee's perspective, while powerful questioning helps them reflect on their performance and identify areas for improvement. Direct communication allows you to articulate your concerns clearly and constructively.

Practical Steps for Confrontational Coaching

1. **Preparation**: Gather all relevant information about the employee's performance. This includes performance metrics, feedback from colleagues, and your observations. Reflect on your feelings and ensure you approach the conversation from a place of constructive intent.

2. **Setting the Stage**: Choose an appropriate time and place for the conversation. Ensure it's private and comfortable, where the employees feel safe expressing themselves.

3. Initiating the Conversation: Start with positive reinforcement. Acknowledge the employee's strengths and contributions before addressing the areas of concern.

This helps in building trust and reducing defensiveness.

4. **Addressing the Issue**: Clearly state the specific performance issues. Use "I" statements to describe your observations and how these issues affect the team or organization. Avoid blaming or using inflammatory language.

5. **Collaborative Problem-Solving**: Engage the employee in finding solutions. Ask for their input on how they can improve, and offer your support. Develop a clear action plan with specific goals and timelines.

6. **Follow up:** Schedule regular check-ins to monitor progress and provide ongoing support. Recognize improvements and continue to offer constructive feedback.

By incorporating these steps, emotional intelligence, and the ICF's ethical principles and core competencies, you can ensure that confrontational coaching becomes a powerful tool for growth and improvement.

ASPIRATIONAL COACHING

The second part of C.A.R.E coaching is learning how to become the aspirational leader that your employees need to ensure they can reach high, stand tall, and perform at their highest levels. Now, you might be saying to yourself, "I'm an experienced coach— getting people to perform is what I do." And while that's all well and good, it isn't just about getting others to perform— you see, it's about getting others to believe in themselves, to trust their abilities, and to hold themselves to a higher standard than anyone else, so they can truly and consistently reach higher, stand taller, and perform more effectively.

Your Duty as A Coach

As a coach, whether you're a professional workplace coach, a life coach, or even a team leader, your job is to help others improve their performance. However, ensuring they strive for excellence every day is a different beast altogether!

Let's take it back to one of our founding fathers— ***Benjamin Franklin***. Did you know that every day, Benjamin Franklin would wake up and follow the same routine? He would wake up at 5 a.m. each morning and begin every day by asking himself the same question, "What good shall I do this day?"

From there, he went on with his day and performed his duties before getting back into bed around 10 p.m. But before he'd go to sleep, he'd ask himself another question, "What good have I done today?" You see, Benjamin Franklin's routine wasn't just about motivating himself— it had to do with character, moral values, and, most importantly, a passion for doing good.

Your duty is to coach your employees into being. You need to teach them how to build character, adopt positive moral values, and use their passion as a propellant in their pursuit of excellence. So, how do you do it?

Embrace Your Passion

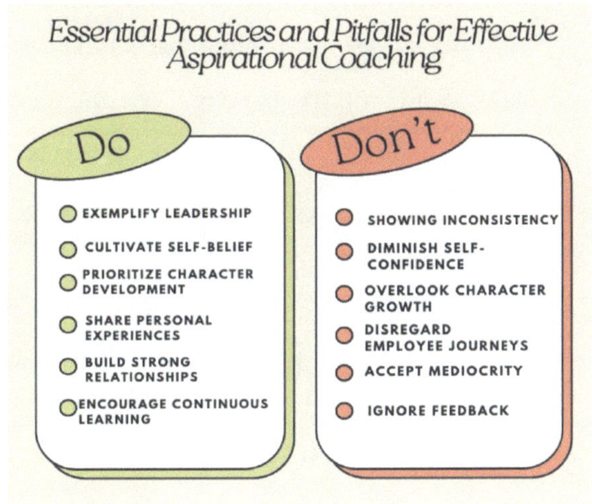

All coaches, regardless of their level of experience, their background, their areas of expertise, or their approach, share one thing in common trait— they're passionate about what they do. If you find yourself unhappy as a coach, it may be time to reevaluate your career choices. However, that is not why you're here.

Coaches exude passion, and this passion is infectious. When you're passionate about your work, your employees feel it too. Your passion drives you to achieve great things because you hold yourself to a higher standard than someone who isn't as dedicated or committed to excellence.

You tend to believe in yourself more than someone who is

disconnected from the work you do. And you tend to think more positively about the impact you can leave on the world.

Connecting with your employees to become the aspirational coach you need to become begins with exuding passion so your employees understand how much their performance means to you and, in turn, to the success of their company.

So, how do you embrace your passions as a coach?

First, you can begin by sharing your journey with your employee or client. Fill them in on the details that brought you to where you are today. Talk about the trials and tribulations, talk about the challenges you needed to overcome, and don't forget to mention the obstacles you needed to find a way to climb over— things like self-doubt, the risk of failing, or the dangers of letting someone down. Then, relate it to their current performance.

Ask them all about their journey. Learn about their interests and the road they took to get to where they are today, empathizing with their struggles, challenges, and worries. From there, you can work to isolate their interests and passions so they can begin to note the little things that brought them to their current position.

Essentially, all you're doing is reminding your employees that they are just as passionate as you are. They don't know how to leverage that passion into productivity, excellence, and success. But that's exactly what you'll continue to work on with them as an aspirational coach.

Practice Really Does Make Perfect

Practice makes perfect— there's no ifs, ands, or buts about it! How exactly does one practice being aspirational? Well, it starts by being aspirational with your employees or your clients. All you can do is develop your connections, build your relationships, and work through issues with employees and clients to truly become the aspirational coach that the C.A.R.E approach demands of you.

It would be best if you coached with a purpose— a coach with a passion, a coach with excellence, and a coach with a strategy. From there, you'll no longer have to try to become the aspirational coach that you want to become— you'll become that coach.

Practical Tips for Aspiring Coaching

1. **Share Your Journey**: First, share your journey with your employee or client. Fill them in on the details that brought you to where you are today. Talk about the trials and tribulations, the challenges you needed to overcome, and the obstacles you needed to climb over— such as self-doubt, the risk of failing, or the dangers of letting someone down. Then, relate it to their current performance.

2. **Learn Their Journey**: Ask them all about their journey. Learn about their interests and the road they took to get to where they are today and empathize with their

struggles, challenges, and worries. From there, you can work to isolate their interests and passions so they can begin to note the little things that brought them to their current position.

3. **Encourage Self-Reflection**: Similar to Benjamin Franklin's practice, encourage your employees to reflect on their daily routines. Have them start their day by setting positive intentions and end their day by reflecting on their accomplishments. This routine can help them stay focused and motivated.

4. **Set High Standards**: Help your employees set high standards for themselves. Please encourage them to aim for excellence in everything they do. This involves setting challenging but achievable goals and continuously striving to improve their performance.

Integrating ICF Core Competencies

ICF's core competencies for aspiring coaching include establishing trust and intimacy with the client, maintaining a coaching presence, and facilitating learning and results. Trust and intimacy are crucial for creating a safe and supportive environment where the employee feels valued and understood. Maintaining a coaching presence involves being fully engaged, present, and focused during coaching sessions, demonstrating confidence in the coaching process, and providing a space for the client to express themselves.

Facilitating learning and results involves helping clients set goals, develop action plans, and stay committed to their objectives. It includes recognizing and celebrating progress and achievements, which reinforces their confidence and motivation.

Practical Steps for Aspirational Coaching

1. Embrace Your Passion

- ❖ **Self-Reflection**: Begin by gaining a deep understanding of your passion for coaching. Reflect on what drives you and why you chose this path. Your genuine enthusiasm will be contagious.

- ❖ **Share Your Journey**: Share your personal story with your employees or clients. Discuss the trials, tribulations, and challenges you have overcome, and relate these experiences to their current situation.

2. Connect Deeply with Employees

❖ **Learn Their Journey**: Take the time to learn about your employees' or clients'
backgrounds. Understand their interests and the paths they've taken, and empathize with their struggles and challenges.

❖ **Empathize and Relate**: Use your understanding of their journey to empathize with their struggles and relate your experiences to theirs, fostering a deeper connection.

3. Encourage Self-Reflection

❖ **Daily Routine**: Encourage employees to start and end their day with self-reflective
questions, similar to Benjamin Franklin's practice. For instance, "What good shall I do this day?" and "What good have I done today?"

❖ **Set Intentions:** Guide them to set positive intentions at the beginning of the day and reflect on their accomplishments at the end of the day. This practice helps maintain focus and motivation.

4. Set High Standards

❖ **Encourage Excellence**: Help employees set high yet achievable standards for themselves. Motivate them to aim for excellence in all their endeavors.

- ❖ **Continuous Improvement**: Emphasize the significance of a mindset of continuous improvement. By setting challenging goals and striving to surpass them, you can inspire your audience to stay motivated and driven in their coaching journey.

5. Foster a Supportive Environment

- ❖ **Trust and Intimacy**: Create a safe and supportive environment where employees feel valued and understood. Building trust and intimacy is crucial for effective coaching.
- ❖ **Coaching Presence**: Maintain a strong coaching presence by being fully engaged, present, and focused during coaching sessions. Demonstrate confidence in the process and provide a space for open expression.

6. Facilitate Learning and Results

- ❖ **Goal Setting**: Assist clients in setting clear, actionable goals and developing concrete action plans to achieve them.
- ❖ **Monitor Progress**: Regularly monitor progress, providing feedback and celebrating achievements to reinforce confidence and motivation.
- ❖ **Adapt and Adjust**: Be flexible and willing to adjust plans as needed, ensuring that the coaching remains effective and relevant.

7. Practice Regularly

- ❖ **Develop Connections**: Continuously work on building strong connections and relationships with your employees or clients.
- ❖ **Resolve Issues:** Actively work through any issues that arise, demonstrating resilience and problem-solving skills.
- ❖ **Coach with Purpose**: Always coach with a clear purpose, passion, and strategy. This ensures you not only meet your goals but also inspire others to reach theirs.

8. Integrate ICF Core Competencies

- ❖ **Establish Trust and Intimacy**: Focus on creating a trustworthy and intimate relationship with your clients, making them feel secure and valued.
- ❖ **Maintain Coaching Presence**: Stay fully engaged and present during sessions, showing confidence and creating a supportive environment for open dialogue.
- ❖ **Facilitate Learning and Results**: Help clients set goals, develop plans, and commit to their objectives, celebrating progress and achievements along the way.

RESILIENCE COACHING

Dr. Carole Pemberton is a resilience expert—an executive coach, a career coach, and a professional development expert. She's also a world-renowned author and a fan-favorite industry speaker. Most importantly, she's known for Resilience Coaching, which is the third part of our C.A.R.E Coaching strategy.

The Oxford English Dictionary defines the word "resilience" as "the capacity to recover quickly from difficulties; toughness." It also describes it as "the ability of a substance or an object to spring back into shape; elasticity." Now, when applied to coaching, each of these definitions' fits in quite well. In fact, and as it relates to coaching, _Dr. Carole Pemberton describes_ resilience as "the capacity to remain flexible in thoughts, behaviors, and emotions under stress."

Throughout one's career, employees are more than likely to undergo a period of prolonged stress. After all, professional lives are not easy to lead and manage— work can and always will take a toll on our mental and physical state. And as unfortunate as it may be, it's simply part of our society. However, it's the

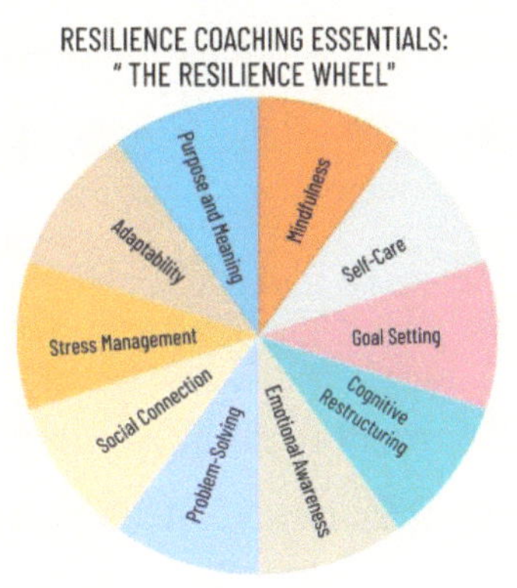

ways we're able to bounce back from stress, recover quickly from difficulties, remain tough, and spring back into shape that makes us effective professionals.

As a coach, you've surely heard it all before— your client has lost their sense of self-confidence, they have trouble making important decisions at work, they've taken on a pessimistic outlook on their work or their company, they don't feel as creative as they once were, they have difficulty managing their emotions in the workplace, and at times, they want to curl up in a ball and hide in their office until the day is over.

As a resilience coach, your job is to address the areas of your employees' or clients' lives where their sense of resilience has taken a hit. It won't be easy, and it certainly will take some time, but once you've tapped into their resilience, you'll end up with a much more productive, positive-minded employee or client.

How Does Resilience Coaching Work?

Interestingly enough, you can technically measure resilience. In fact, it's often used as a powerful psychometric. So, for instance, if you score high on self-confidence, it may lead you to believe you will always remain self-confident in yourself and your abilities. However, that may not be the case since the metric fails to take circumstances, situations, and changing environments into account.

As a resilience coach, your job is to use the psychometrics of resilience to your advantage. More than likely, your employees were— at least at one point— confident in their abilities.

Regardless of the actual metric, you can count on their previous high score in self-confidence to help you get them back to where they need to be. Dr. Carole Pemberton recommends you do this by asking your employee the following questions:

What is different in this situation?

First, resilience coaching requires you to examine both the current situation and similar situations in the past. Talk to your employee or your client about how this situation is different from similar situations that have already occurred in the past. Ask them to point out and identify a similar situation and ask them how they responded. From there, you can begin to discuss the differences between each situation, how a different response would have been more beneficial in the past and how that can be applied in their current situation.

What is the narrative you've created about yourself due to this new situation?

Try to get inside the mind of your employee or your client. If they've really lost their self-confidence, then it's safe to say they've probably created a narrative about themselves or their abilities due to this new situation. For example, thoughts like "I'm not good at my job. I really failed at this task and let my boss down. I used to be good at __________, but I'm not the same person I used to be," are common and are the likely culprit for their loss of self-confidence.

How Big Is the Resilience Gap?

The resilience gap refers to the difference between the level of self-confidence your employee or client felt prior to the situation and the level of self-confidence they have after it's already unfolded. You need to do your best to determine just how big this gap is. Suppose the situation resulted in a minor loss of confidence and could be passed off as a hiccup in an otherwise positive professional career. In that case, you can alter your approach to help your employee work through the situation.

On the other hand, if the situation has left your employee or client demoralized, depressed, anxious, or all of the above, you'll certainly have your work cut out for you. Depending on the nature of the situation, you may be required to apply the first two parts of the C.A.R.E Coaching strategy to help your employee find that sense of resiliency again.

How can we develop a new narrative?

It's important to remain open and honest with your employee or client throughout the resilience coaching process. You want them to have a say in where they go from here—after all, it's their life and their career, right? So, ask them about the narrative they really want for themselves. Try to establish that the narrative of this new situation is inaccurate, unrealistic, and certainly not in line with their past achievements.

You can work together to write a brand-new narrative for them— one that will strategically position them to receive the confidence boost they need and deserve.

How can we enact that new narrative?

At this point, it's time to work with your employee or client to develop a real strategy and plan for implementing that new narrative. This plan can include a wide range of tips and tactics to ensure situations like those that have unfolded previously in their careers either don't happen again or can be addressed differently.

Integrating ICF Core Competencies and Ethical Principles

The ICF outlines several core competencies and ethical principles that are particularly relevant to resilience coaching. These include:

- ❖ Establishing Trust and Intimacy: Creating a safe and supportive environment where clients feel respected and understood.
- ❖ Coaching Presence: Being fully present and flexible during coaching interactions.
- ❖ Active Listening: Completely focusing on what the client is saying and understanding their perspective.
- ❖ Powerful Questioning: Asking questions that reveal the information needed for maximum benefit to the coaching relationship and the client.
- ❖ Creating Awareness: Integrating and accurately evaluating multiple sources of information and making interpretations that help the client gain awareness.

By integrating these competencies, you can help your clients develop resilience more effectively. Establishing trust allows clients to feel safe discussing their vulnerabilities, while powerful questioning can help them gain insights into ways to strengthen and increase their resilience.

Practical Steps for Resilience Coaching

1. Understand and Define Resilience

- ❖ Define Resilience: Begin by understanding and defining resilience in the context of your coaching. Use Oxford's definitions: the capacity to recover quickly from difficulties (toughness) and the ability to spring back into shape (elasticity).
- ❖ Explain Resilience: Coaching: Clarify for your clients that resilience coaching focuses on helping them remain flexible in thoughts, behaviors, and emotions under stress, as described by Dr. Carole Pemberton.

2. Assess the Current Situation

- ❖ Evaluate the Situation: Discuss the current situation with your client and help them to compare it to past experiences. Work together to identify what is different this time.
- ❖ Understand the Impact: Determine how the situation has affected their self-confidence, decision-making, creativity, and emotional management.

3. Identify and Address Negative Narratives

- ❖ Explore Self-Narratives: Ask your client to articulate the narrative they have created about themselves due to the new situation. This could include negative self-talk and loss of self-confidence.

❖ Challenge Negative Thoughts: Help your client recognize that these narratives are often inaccurate and unrealistic. Use probing questions to challenge and then guide them through reframing these thoughts.

4. Measure the Resilience Gap

❖ Determine the Gap: Assess the difference between their previous level of self-confidence and their current state. This resilience gap will guide your approach.

❖ Tailor Your Approach: Depending on the size of the gap, customize your coaching strategy. A minor gap may require simple adjustments, while a significant gap might necessitate a more comprehensive approach.

5. Develop a New Narrative

❖ Co-create a New Story: Work with your client to develop a new, positive narrative about their abilities and potential. Ensure this narrative aligns with their past achievements and future goals.

❖ Empower the Client: Encourage your client to take an active role in creating this new narrative, reinforcing their sense of agency and self-efficacy.

6. Implement the New Narrative

- ❖ Create a Strategy: Develop a clear plan with actionable steps your client can follow to embody their new narrative. This should include specific goals, strategies, and practices to maintain resilience.
- ❖ Monitor Progress: Review their progress regularly and make adjustments as necessary. Celebrate successes and encourage them to learn from setbacks to continuously build resilience.

7. Integrate ICF Core Competencies

- ❖ Establish Trust and Intimacy: Create a safe, supportive environment where clients feel respected and understood.
- ❖ Maintain Coaching Presence: Be fully present and flexible during coaching sessions, adapting to the client's needs.
- ❖ Practice Active Listening: Focus completely on the client's words to gain a deep understanding of their perspective.
- ❖ Ask Powerful Questions: Use questions that uncover critical information and insights for the client's benefit.
- ❖ Create Awareness: Integrate multiple sources of information to help clients gain a deeper understanding of their resilience.

8. Continuously Develop Resilience

- ❖ Encourage Ongoing Reflection: Promote regular self-reflection and assessment to help clients stay aware of their resilience levels.

- ❖ Build a Support Network: Help clients identify and cultivate a support network of colleagues, mentors, and friends who can provide encouragement and perspective.
- ❖ Promote Self-Care: Emphasize the importance of physical and mental self-care practices to sustain resilience over time.

EMERGING LIFE COACHING

The job of a coach isn't simply to work with employees and clients to ensure they exhibit excellence in their professional lives— it's to ensure they can apply the skills, strategies, and tactics they've learned to exhibit excellence in life, too! Every coach is a life coach because, for many of us and many of our clients, our professional lives often make up at least 50% of who we are— for others, it's closer to everything they are and how they define and identify themselves.

As a coach, I can truly say that coaching is my life. I have a family whom I love, I have friends whom I love, and I have a business that I love— but I also love to coach. I love to help others, I love to help others strive for excellence, and I love to provide services to benefit others.

Since you're reading this book, you likely want to grow your skills, develop your abilities as a coach, and learn how to connect with your employees and clients on a deeper level than ever before. Do you know what this tells me? It tells me that coaching is your life, too!

You Can Be More Than a Coach

Coaching is an overarching term that can include everything from a teacher to a leader to an advisor. But most importantly, coaching encompasses something that goes beyond professional development and relates to personal development.

You can become a mentor. A mentor is someone who teaches others both the tangible and the intangible—they teach their employees or their clients how to do a job or learn a skill, but they also teach them how to act, think, feel, and, in essence, live.

As mentioned earlier, your passion is infectious— it's contagious, and it will certainly rub off on your employees and your clients— and that's 100% true. When your employees and clients work with you, they'll pick up on the way you conduct your work. They'll take note of the things you say, the way you approach situations, the thoughts you share with them, and even your mannerisms. They'll pick up on your ability to listen, connect, empathize, suggest, point out, identify, discuss, and, most importantly, care.

As the fourth part of the C.A.R.E Coaching strategy, your goal is to become more than just a coach. It would be best if you become an emerging life coach, someone your clients can look to for guidance in their personal lives and help them achieve their goals at work and beyond.

Developing Soft Skills

Have you ever heard of soft skills? Soft skills are those intangibles I mentioned earlier—they can't necessarily be taught, but they can be learned through example. As an emerging life coach, you can make more of an impact than just boosting the workplace performance of your employees and clients. You can help them develop the soft skills they can use in all aspects of their lives.

These skills include a combination of communication skills, social skills, people skills, listening skills, personality traits, emotional comprehension, emotional intelligence, and so much more. While you may not realize it, all of these skills come into play solely through the work you do.

This means you need to be aware of the ways in which you exhibit all of these skills throughout your coaching sessions. When you connect with your employees and clients, exhibiting the right communication skills is of the utmost importance. This means putting things like respect, honesty, trust, and transparency at the top of your list! In the same breath, giving them tips and tricks on how to handle social situations is important. You can ask them about things they've said during meetings, interactions they've had with their superiors or team members, and how they respond when facing feedback or criticism. From there, you can suggest how you'd respond, or you can recommend a different approach.

But whatever you do, rest assured that your words will be heard and trusted because you've already established the level of trust that qualifies you to be a mentor. That trust makes others rely on you as a mentor and see you as a mentor.

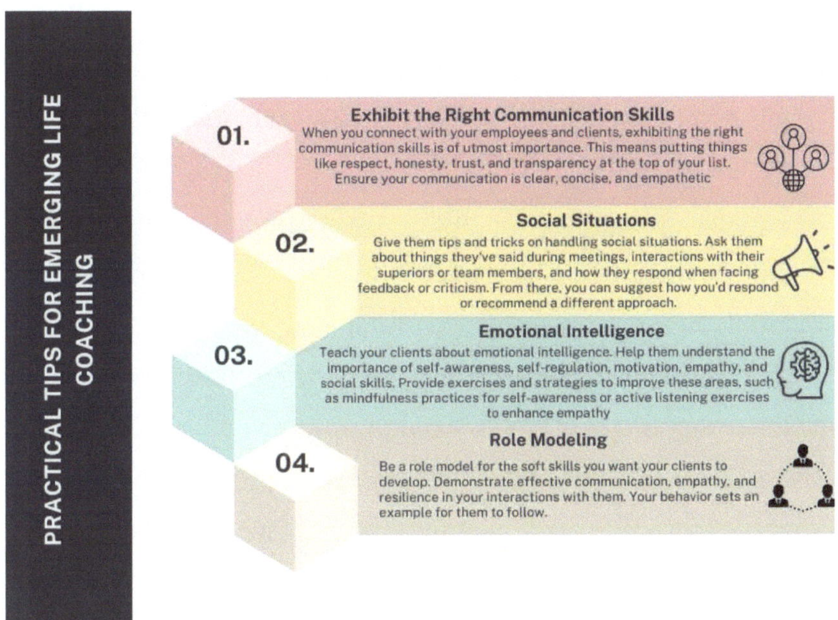

Integrating ICF Core Competencies and Ethical Principles

ICF core competencies relevant to emerging life coaching include:

- ❖ **Establishing Trust and Intimacy with the Client**: Creating a safe, supportive environment where the client feels valued and respected.

- ❖ **Maintaining a Coaching Presence**: Being intentional

and creating spontaneous relationships with clients, employing a style that is open, flexible, and confident.

- ❖ **Communicating Effectively**: Using language that has the greatest positive impact on the client, listening actively, and asking powerful questions.
- ❖ **Facilitating Learning and Results**: Helping clients create a vision and develop strategies to achieve their goals, promoting self-discovery, and facilitating client growth.

Ethical principles include maintaining confidentiality, promoting the client's best interests, and adhering to the highest standards of integrity and professionalism.

As the final part of the C.A.R.E Coaching strategy, becoming the emerging life coach, you need to ensure you have everything you need to use passion, excellence, and strategy to develop effective employees and become the most successful coach you can be. Prior to concluding, let's look at the ICF and core competencies to sharpen our skills further to achieve the next level of coaching excellence.

Practical Steps for Emerging Life Coaching

1. Exhibit the Right Communication Skills

- ❖ **Prioritize Key Traits**: Focus on respect, honesty, trust, and transparency in all interactions.
- ❖ **Clear Communication**: Ensure your messages are clear, concise, and empathetic.
- ❖ **Active Listening**: Practice active listening to fully

understand your clients' perspectives and needs.

2. Handle Social Situations

- ❖ **Offer Practical Tips**: Guide managing social interactions, including meetings and feedback sessions.
- ❖ **Discuss Real Scenarios**: Ask clients about their experiences in social situations and offer alternative approaches or improvements.
- ❖ **Role-play scenarios:** Conduct role-playing exercises to practice effective communication and social skills in a safe environment.

3. Develop Emotional Intelligence

- ❖ **Teach Core Components**: Educate clients on self-awareness, self-regulation, motivation, empathy, and social skills.
- ❖ **Provide Exercises**: Use mindfulness practices for self-awareness, active listening exercises to enhance empathy, and other activities to build emotional intelligence.
- ❖ **Monitor Progress:** Regularly check in on their emotional development and adjust strategies as needed.

4. Be a Role Model

- ❖ **Demonstrate Soft Skills**: Exhibit effective communication, empathy, and resilience in your interactions.

❖ **Lead by Example:** Show others how to handle challenges, maintain professionalism, and build strong relationships.

❖ **Reflect on Actions**: After interactions, discuss what you did well and what could be improved to provide a learning opportunity for your clients.

5. Establish Trust and Intimacy

❖ **Create a Safe Environment**: Ensure clients feel valued and respected by being supportive and non-judgmental.

❖ **Build Rapport:** Take the time to understand your clients' backgrounds and goals, fostering a deeper connection.

❖ **Confidentiality:** Always maintain confidentiality to build and sustain trust.

6. Maintain a Coaching Presence

❖ **Be Fully Present**: Stay focused and engaged during coaching sessions.

❖ **Adapt Flexibly:** Be open, flexible, and confident in your coaching style to meet the evolving needs of your clients.

❖ **Spontaneous Relationships**: Encourage natural, authentic interactions to strengthen the coaching relationship.

7. Communicate Effectively

❖ **Use Positive Language**: Employ language that has

the greatest positive impact on the client.

- ❖ **Active Listening:** Listen actively to understand the client's concerns, needs, and goals.
- ❖ **Ask Powerful Questions**: Use powerful questioning to elicit insightful responses and promote self-discovery.

8. Facilitate Learning and Results

- ❖ **Create a Vision**: Help clients articulate a clear vision for their future.
- ❖ **Develop Strategies:** Work with clients to create actionable strategies to achieve their goals.
- ❖ **Promote Self-Discovery**: Encourage clients to explore their strengths and areas for growth.
- ❖ **Facilitate Growth:** Support clients in their journey of personal and professional development.

9. Integrate ICF Core Competencies and Ethical Principles

- ❖ **Trust and Intimacy**: Establish a safe, supportive environment where clients feel valued.
- ❖ **Coaching Presence:** Be mindful, stay focused, stay present, remain present, be intentional, adaptable, and confident in your coaching style.
- ❖ **Effective Communication**: Use impactful language, listen actively, and ask powerful questions.
- ❖ **Facilitate Learning and Results:** Help clients create a vision, develop strategies, and promote self-

discovery.

- ❖ **Ethical Standards**: Maintain confidentiality, promote the client's best interests, and adhere to the highest standards of integrity and professionalism.

10. Continuous Improvement

- ❖ **Reflect and Adapt**: Continuously reflect on your coaching practices and seek feedback for improvement.
- ❖ **Professional Development**: Engage in ongoing learning and professional development to stay updated with coaching best practices and trends.
- ❖ **Network with Peers:** Connect with other coaches to share experiences, gain insights, and foster a supportive community.

ICF Ethical Principles and Core Competencies

To be an effective and superb coach using the CARE method, it's essential to adhere to the International Coaching Federation (ICF) ethical principles and core competencies. These guidelines not only ensure the highest standards of coaching but also help in fostering trust and respect between the coach and the client.

ICF Ethical Principles

1) **Integrity**: Conducting oneself with honesty and transparency in all interactions. As a coach, it's important to maintain high ethical standards and ensure your actions align with your words.

2) **Confidentiality:** Respect your client's privacy and maintain the confidentiality of all information shared during coaching sessions. This principle is critical in building trust and creating a safe space for clients to express themselves.

3) **Professionalism**: Demonstrating respect, empathy, and understanding towards clients while maintaining professional boundaries. This includes being punctual, prepared, and fully present during coaching sessions.

4) **Conflict of Interest**: Avoid situations where personal interests may conflict with the client's interests. It's

important to disclose any potential conflicts of interest and act in the best interest of the client at all times.

5) **Continuous Development**: Committing to ongoing personal and professional development to enhance your coaching skills and stay current with best practices in the field.

ICF Core Competencies

1. **Setting the Foundation:**
    - ❖ **Meeting Ethical Guidelines and Professional Standards**: Understanding and consistently applying coaching ethics and standards of coaching.
    - ❖ **Establishing the Coaching Agreement**: Clearly articulating the coaching process, including roles, responsibilities, and expectations.

2. **Co-Creating the Relationship:**
    - ❖ **Establishing Trust and Intimacy with the Client:** Creating a safe and supportive environment where the client feels valued and respected.
    - ❖ **Coaching Presence:** Being fully present and mindful, fully alert, focused, creating spontaneous relationships with clients, and employing an open, flexible, and confident style.

3. **Communicating Effectively:**
    - ❖ **Active Listening:** Completely focusing on what

the client is saying and understanding their perspective.

- ❖ **Powerful Questioning**: Asking questions that reveal the information needed for maximum benefit to the coaching relationship and the client.
- ❖ **Direct Communication**: Communicating effectively during coaching sessions and using language that has the greatest positive impact on the client.

4. **Facilitating Learning and Results:**

- ❖ **Creating Awareness**: Integrating and accurately evaluating multiple sources of information and making interpretations that help the client gain awareness.
- ❖ **Designing Actions**: Working with the client to create opportunities for ongoing learning during coaching and in work/life situations and for taking new actions that will most effectively lead to agreed-upon coaching results.
- ❖ **Planning and Goal Setting**: Developing and maintaining an effective coaching plan with the client.
- ❖ **Managing Progress and Accountability**: We must maintain a focus on what is important for the client and give them the responsibility for taking action.

Applying ICF Principles and Competencies to the CARE Method

By integrating ICF principles and core competencies with the CARE method, you can ensure a holistic and ethical approach to coaching that not only focuses on immediate performance but also fosters long-term personal and professional growth.

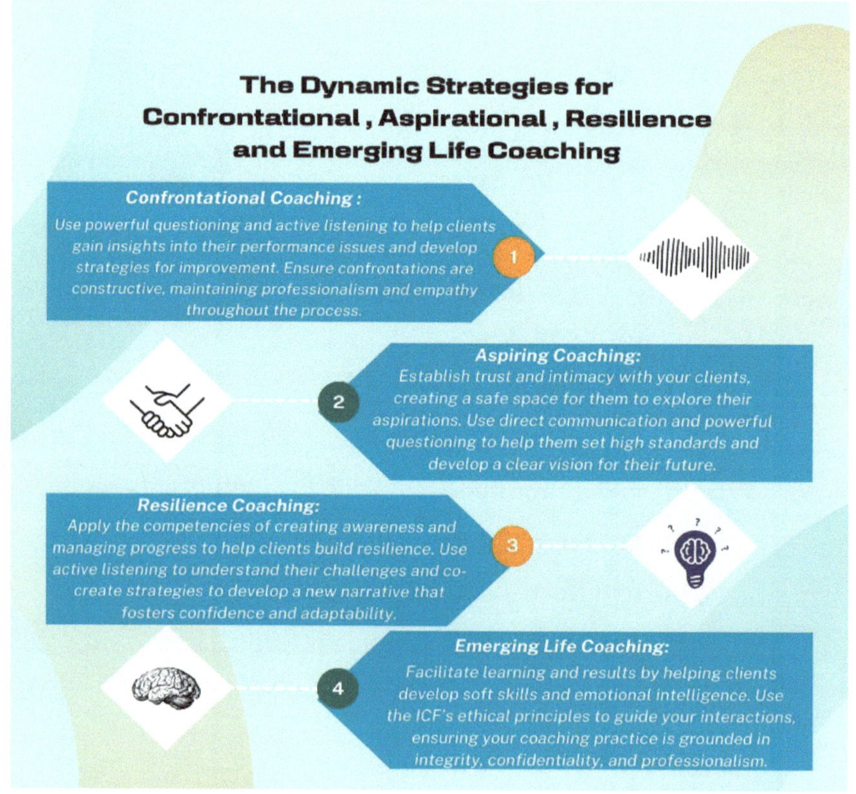

By combining the CARE method with the ICF's ethical principles and core competencies, you can become an effective and superb coach capable of addressing the unique challenges of today's workforce and serving today's young people. This integrated approach ensures your coaching practice is not only impactful but also ethical and sustainable, fostering trust and respect between you and your clients.

Through this comprehensive guide, you now have a wealth of knowledge on transformative coaching for every generation. The CARE method, enriched with insights from the ICF, provides you with the tools and strategies needed to excel as a coach, mentor, and leader. Embrace this approach, and you will undoubtedly make a significant difference in the lives of your clients, helping them achieve excellence in their professional and personal lives.

CONCLUSION

Embracing the C.A.R.E. Model

Whether you're a coach in the healthcare industry, human resources, professional services, or any other field, your role is crucial and integral to ensuring that employees perform at their best to drive organizational success. As a coach, you hold the incredible responsibility of imparting your knowledge, experience, and expertise to help individuals become the best professionals they can be.

This book has equipped you with the C.A.R.E. Model. This innovative approach combines the power of passion, excellence, and strategy to develop effective employees and holistic individuals, regardless of their industry. This transformative method is designed to address the unique challenges faced by today's generations, providing a comprehensive framework for impactful coaching.

Throughout my nearly 30-year career, I've drawn from my military, leadership, and entrepreneurial experiences to become the best possible coach, leader, and mentor. I have witnessed the digital transformation, seen promising students struggle to find employment, and watched professionals leave their careers due to various challenges. These experiences have shaped the C.A.R.E. Model, a strategy that encapsulates the lessons learned from both successes and failures.

The C.A.R.E. Model—Confrontational Coaching, Aspirational Coaching, Resilience Coaching, and Emerging Life Coaching—offers a structured yet flexible approach to coaching that addresses the dynamic needs of modern professionals. It emphasizes the importance of constructive confrontation, the power of aspiration, the necessity of resilience, and the value of life coaching beyond the workplace.

As coaches, our impact goes beyond professional development. We have the opportunity to inspire, motivate, and transform lives. Remember the wise words of ***Theodore Roosevelt: "People don't care how much you know until they know how much you care"*** (Roosevelt, 1903). This quote underscores the essence of the C.A.R.E. Model—showing genuine care and empathy is the foundation of effective coaching.

By embracing this model, you are not just improving workplace performance; you are fostering a culture of care, trust, and excellence. You are empowering individuals to overcome challenges, reach their highest potential, and lead fulfilling lives both professionally and personally.

Are you ready to put the C.A.R.E. Model into practice? Are you prepared to be the coach who not only imparts knowledge but also demonstrates profound care and commitment to your client's success? The journey of transformative coaching starts with you. Embrace the C.A.R.E. Model, and let it guide you in making a lasting impact on those you coach.

Thank you for joining me on this journey. May the C.A.R.E. Model inspire you to coach with passion, lead with excellence, and transform lives with every interaction.

In His love and grace,

Steven L. Jordan Sr., Ph.D., Ed.D. (AKA: Dr. J)

Workbook for Mastering "The CARE Method: Transformative Coaching for Every Generation"

This workbook is designed to accompany "The CARE Method" by Dr. Steven Jordan, Sr., Ph.D., Ed.D., and provides a practical framework for applying the principles and techniques discussed in the book. It aims to inspire, motivate, educate, and provide revelations to help you master the knowledge contained within the book. Each section includes exercises, reflections, and action plans.

Section 1: Confrontational Coaching

Understanding Constructive Confrontation

Exercise 1: Identify a situation where constructive confrontation is needed in your coaching practice. Describe the situation and your intended approach.

____

____

____

____

____

____

Reflection: What challenges do you foresee in this confrontation, and how can you prepare to handle them constructively?

____

____

____

____

____

____

Practical Steps for Confrontational Coaching

Exercise 2: Use the provided framework to plan a confrontation session with an employee or client.

- Preparation:
- Gather relevant performance data.
- Reflect on your emotions and intentions.
- Initiation:
- Start with positives.
- Use "I" statements.
- Maintain a calm demeanor.
- Collaboration:
- Engage the employee in problem-solving.
- Develop an action plan together.
- Follow-Up:
- Monitor progress.

- Provide ongoing support.

The Role of Emotional Intelligence

Exercise 3: Assess your emotional intelligence using Goleman's key components. Identify areas for improvement.

____

____

____

____

____

____

____

Reflection: How can you enhance your self-awareness, self-regulation, motivation, empathy, and social skills to improve your confrontational coaching?

____

____

____

____

____

____

____

Section 2: Aspirational Coaching

Becoming an Aspirational Leader

Exercise 4: Reflect on your journey as a coach and write a narrative that highlights your trials, tribulations, and triumphs.

____

____

____

____

____

____

____

Reflection: How does your journey inspire your coaching practice? How can you use your story to motivate your clients?

____

____

____

____

____

____

____

Encouraging Self-Reflection

Exercise 5: Develop a daily routine inspired by Benjamin Franklin's practice. Set intentions each morning and reflect each evening.

Reflection: How does this routine impact your coaching effectiveness and personal growth?

Setting High Standards

Exercise 6: Help an employee or client set high standards and achievable goals.

Action Plan: Outline specific, measurable, achievable, relevant, and time-bound (SMART) goals.

Follow-up: Create a timeline for regular check-ins and adjustments.

Section 3: Resilience Coaching

Defining and Measuring Resilience

Exercise 7: Assess the resilience of an employee or client using the provided psychometric tools.

Reflection: Identify key areas where resilience needs to be developed.

____

____

____

____

____

____

____

Developing a New Narrative

Exercise 8: Work with your client to rewrite their self-narrative.

- Steps:
- Identify negative narratives.
- Develop a positive, empowering narrative.
- Create an action plan to enact the new narrative.

Practical Steps for Resilience Coaching

Exercise 9: Implement a resilience coaching session using the outlined steps.

Reflection: How did the session impact your client's confidence and resilience?

Section 4: Emerging Life Coaching

Developing Soft Skills

Exercise 10: Identify key soft skills needed by your client and develop a plan to enhance these skills through coaching.

____

____

____

____

____

____

Reflection: How can improving these soft skills benefit your client's professional and personal life?

____

____

____

____

____

Establishing Trust and Intimacy

Exercise 11: Create a safe and supportive environment for your clients.

Action Plan: Implement strategies to build trust and intimacy, such as maintaining confidentiality and showing genuine care.

____

____

____

____

____

____

Facilitating Learning and Results

Exercise 12: Help your client set a clear vision and actionable strategies for their goals.

Reflection: How does facilitating learning and results enhance your effectiveness as a life coach?

____

____

____

____

____

____

____

Integrating ICF Core Competencies and Ethical Principles

Applying ICF Principles

Exercise 13: Reflect on how you can integrate ICF ethical principles and core competencies into your coaching practice.

____

____

____

____

____

____

____

Action Plan: Develop specific strategies to apply these principles in your daily coaching interactions.

____

____

____

____

____

____

____

Continuous Improvement

Personal and Professional Development

Exercise 14: Set personal goals for continuous improvement in your coaching practice.

____

____

____

____

____

____

Reflection: How can ongoing learning and professional development enhance your coaching skills?

____

____

____

____

____

____

Networking with Peers

Exercise 15: Identify opportunities to connect with other coaches. Plan how to share experiences and gain insights.

____

Action Plan: Develop a schedule for attending coaching conferences, joining professional groups, and participating in peer review sessions.

Conclusion

Reflect on your journey through this workbook and the knowledge gained from "The CARE Method." How has this process transformed your approach to coaching? What are your next steps for implementing the CARE model in your professional and personal life?

By actively engaging with this workbook, you can deepen your understanding and application of the CARE method, enhance your effectiveness as a coach and significantly impact the lives of those you coach.

Caprino, K. (n.d.). Critical steps to fearless confrontation. Forbes. https://www.forbes.com/sites/kathycaprino/2013/11/04/5-critical-steps-to-fearless- confrontation/#24f7cff82b4d

McDonough, M. (n.d.). Aspirational coaching: reaching toward your highest and best. Kripalu. https://kripalu.org/resources/aspirational-coaching-reaching-toward-your-highest-and-best

Oxford University Press. (n.d.). Resilience. In OED.com dictionary. https://www.oed.com/dictionary/resilience_n?tl=true

Pemberton, C. (n.d.). Resilience coaching. Carole Pemberton. https://carolepemberton.co.uk/resilience-coaching/

Purbasari, A. (2016, Sept. 16). I followed Benjamin Franklin's daily schedule for a week, and the most rewarding part was also the most difficult. Business Insider. https://www.businessinsider.com/benjamin-franklin-daily-routine-experiment-2016-8

Scott, P. (n.d.). The power of constructive confrontation. Forbes. https://cmoe.com/blog/the-power-of-constructive-confrontation/

Sturt, D. & Nordstrom, T. (2016, Jan. 13). True or false? Employees today only stay one or two years. Forbes. https://www.forbes.com/sites/davidsturt/2016/01/13/true-or-false-employees-today-only-stay- one-or-two-years/#161b6a06b4c7

Taylor, J. (2020, August 29). Twenty great quotes on coaching. Jane Taylor | Realignment and Wellbeing Coaching | Transition Coaching | Gold Coast. https://www.habitsforwellbeing.com/20-great-quotes-on-coaching/

References

Acknowledgment

As we conclude *The C.A.R.E. Method: Transformative Coaching for Every Generation*, my heart overflows with profound gratitude for the journey we have embarked on together. This book is more than just a method for offering transformative coaching; it is a testament to the power of faith, the strength of community, and the boundless love of our Heavenly Father.

Honor and Glory to God

First and foremost, all honor and glory go to God, whose unwavering love and grace have been my guiding light. His presence in my life has provided strength, healing, and inspiration. I am deeply thankful for His miraculous works and the countless ways He has shown His faithfulness.

Appreciation to My Family

I extend my heartfelt appreciation to my beloved wife and prayer partner, Dr. L. Paulette Jordan. Her unwavering support, love, and prayers have been the cornerstone of my spiritual journey. Also, thank you for your editing and partnering with me to make this book happen. You are the greatest! To my children—Lakisha Hyatt, CEO of Connecticut Valley Hospital; Dr. Pauletta Jordan, Resident at the University of Pennsylvania Memorial Hospital; and our son, Steven Jr.— thank you for your continued love and support.

To my father, Joseph Jackson, whom I love dearly for keeping me on my knees, praying, and growing in Jesus, thank you, Dad. You are the best! I also express my gratitude to David Hyatt, my son-in-law, who is my son, for always supporting and praying for me.

Additionally, I want to acknowledge my spiritual son, who is also a son, Chaplain (COL) John Paul Smith, Ph.D., for his continual love and support. To our grandchildren, Eden Hyatt and Elijah Hyatt, your love and joy are invaluable blessings.

Gratitude for Friends and Community

I also want to express my deep appreciation to my best friends, Dr. Gary Patterson, Pastor Be Louis Colleton, Dr. Carl D. Brown, Chaplain Tex Wilson, and Brother Gennaire Harris, for always encouraging and supporting me in prayer, friendship, and love. Your steadfast support has been a pillar of strength for me, and I am grateful for your unwavering faith and friendship. I am grateful to my Church family and Bishop A. Ladell Thomas, Jr., Ph.D., for your ongoing support and love.

Thanks to the Readers

To all the readers of this book, I extend my deepest appreciation. Your commitment to seeking a deeper connection with God through these prayers is a testament to your faith and dedication. I pray that this book has been a source of inspiration, encouragement, and spiritual growth for you.

Encouragement for the Future

As you continue your professional journey, I encourage you to trust in your abilities and the knowledge you've gained. Embrace every situation with confidence, knowing that you can overcome challenges and achieve great success. When faced with obstacles, remember that perseverance and resilience are key to navigating through difficult times.

May you continue to seek growth and excellence in all that you do. Let your commitment to continuous improvement be unwavering and remain open to learning and personal development. Trust in the process and allow your wisdom and experiences to guide your steps.

Guiding Principle

"People don't care how much you know until they know how much you care." - Theodore Roosevelt. Let this principle be a guiding light in your professional life, reminding you to lead with empathy and compassion. By showing genuine care and understanding, you can build strong, meaningful connections and inspire others to reach their full potential.

May your journey be filled with opportunities for growth, success, and fulfillment. Embrace the C.A.R.E. Model, and let it empower you to make a positive impact in the workplace and beyond.

As you continue your spiritual journey, I encourage you to trust in the Lord with all your heart and lean not on your understanding. In every situation, walk by faith, believing that God is with you, guiding and protecting you. When faced with challenges, remember that God's love and grace are boundless, and His healing power is real.

May you continue to seek Him diligently, knowing that He rewards those who do. Let your faith be unwavering, your prayers be fervent, and your heart be open to the divine connection that transforms lives. Trust in God's plan for your life and allow His wisdom to guide your steps.

Dedication

This book is dedicated to my dear friend, prayer warrior partner, and mentor, Chaplain (COL) Dr. Sir Walter Scott. His legacy of faith, prayer, and mentorship continues to inspire and guide me. May his memory be a blessing and his life a testament to the power of prayer and faith, coupled with his passion for coaching, counseling, and teaching at all levels.

May God bless you abundantly, fill your heart with His peace, and lead you on a path of righteousness and love. Thank you for joining me on this journey of C.A.R.E. coaching. Together, let us continue to seek knowledge and serve with excellence in a changing generation.

In His love and grace,

Steven L. Jordan Sr., Ph.D., Ed.D. (AKA: Dr. J)

About the Author

Dr. Steven L. Jordan Sr., Ph.D., Ed.D. (AKA: Dr. J) is a compassionate and dedicated former pastor and chaplain with over 30 years of ministry experience. His deep commitment to prayer and spiritual guidance has touched countless lives, reflecting his unwavering devotion to caring for souls and building the Kingdom of God.

A retired senior military officer with three decades of service, Dr. Jordan has excelled as an educator, pastoral therapist, theologian, administrator, and executive coach. His extensive experience in strategic leadership, academic influence, and personal development spans both public and private sectors. Dr. Jordan's multifaceted expertise includes human resource development, operations, spiritual growth, pastoral care, strategic planning, business development, and project management.

As an award-winning entrepreneur and the owner of Dr. J Enterprises LLC, Dr. Jordan is renowned for his exceptional leadership and inspirational skills. He is a sought-after consultant and coach specializing in enhancing leadership abilities, boosting self-awareness, building confidence, improving decision-making, and fostering effective communication. His unique blend of military discipline and pastoral care equips him to guide individuals and organizations toward achieving their highest potential.

Dr. Jordan's life's work is a testament to his passion for ministry and his dedication to helping others grow spiritually and personally. Whether through his writings, teachings, or one-on-one coaching, Dr. Jordan remains committed to making a positive.